Table of Contents

The Basics of Economics

Real-Life Skills School Forgot to Teach You

James T. Blake

About the Book

Money is something everyone uses, but few people are ever *taught* how it really works.

Schools may teach math or history, but not how to budget, read a payslip, invest wisely, or avoid debt traps. And yet, these are the skills that shape our everyday lives.

This book was created to fill that gap. It's a simple, no-fluff guide to understanding how money actually works in today's world: from cash and digital payments to taxes, credit, investing, and planning for your future.

Whether you're a student, a recent graduate, or just someone trying to make sense of personal finance, this book breaks everything down in plain language. No complicated charts, no business jargon, just real-world explanations and examples that make sense.

You'll learn how to:

- Manage your income and expenses without stress.
- Build and protect good credit.
- Understand taxes, insurance, and loans.
- Make smart financial choices every day.
- Plan ahead for big goals like buying a home or retiring comfortably.

Every chapter is designed to help you feel more confident and in control of your money. By the end, you'll see that personal finance isn't just for experts. It's something *you* can master, one smart decision at a time.

Because when you understand money, you don't just survive, but you thrive.

1.

Understanding Money Basics

What Money Is and How It Works Today

Money is one of those things that everyone uses, but very few people actually stop to think about. At its core, money is just a tool. It's a way for people to exchange value with each other. Long ago, people traded goods directly: a farmer might trade a basket of apples for a pair of shoes made by a cobbler. This was called barter, and it worked fine in small communities, but it quickly became complicated. What if the cobbler didn't need apples? What if the farmer wanted shoes later but had nothing to trade at that moment? That's where money came in.

Money became the middle step in trade. Instead of swapping apples for shoes, the farmer could sell the apples for money, and later use that money to buy shoes when needed. Money solved the problem of timing and made trade far more flexible. But money itself is not valuable because of the material it's made from; it's valuable because people agree it is. A paper bill or a coin doesn't have much use on its own, as you can't eat it or wear it. Its power comes from the trust that others will accept it in exchange for goods and services.

Today, money comes in several forms. The most familiar is physical cash: the paper bills and coins in your wallet. Cash is simple and immediate. If you hand someone a $10 bill, you instantly transfer value with no need for technology, banks, or systems in between. But as the world has become more connected and digital, physical cash is used less often, especially by younger generations.

Most money today actually exists in digital form. When you see your bank balance on an app, that number represents how much money the bank owes you, but the cash itself isn't sitting in a vault with your name on it. Instead, it's part of a digital system where banks, companies, and governments keep track of who owns what. You might get paid directly into your account, spend money using a debit card, or send money online. All of these are digital transactions, and they are the most common form of money movement today.

Credit adds another layer. When you use a credit card, you are not spending your own money right away. You are borrowing money from a credit card company or bank, with the promise to pay it back later. If you pay on time, it works almost like digital cash. But if you delay, the lender charges interest, which is how they make their profit. Credit makes it possible to spend money you don't yet have, which can be useful but also dangerous if not managed carefully.

In recent years, cryptocurrency has entered the picture. Cryptocurrencies like Bitcoin and Ethereum are forms of digital money that don't rely on traditional banks or governments to exist. Instead, they are built on technology called blockchain, which records transactions in a decentralized way. Some people see crypto as the future of money, while others view it as too unstable or risky to use in everyday life. Whether or not it replaces traditional money, cryptocurrencies have already changed how people think about value and financial systems.

What ties all these forms of money together is the same principle that has always been true: money only works because people agree to trust it. A dollar bill, a bank balance, a credit card limit, or even a piece of digital code only matters if others accept it in exchange for goods and services. Understanding this idea, that money is ultimately built on trust, is the first step in learning how to manage it wisely.

Inflation & Purchasing Power

When people talk about the economy, one of the most common words you'll hear is "inflation." It sounds technical, but it simply means that prices go up over time. Inflation is the reason your grandparents might say, "Back in my day, a candy bar cost a dime," while today the same candy bar costs a dollar or more. It's not that candy has become magically more valuable, but it's that the money itself buys less than it used to.

Purchasing power is the flip side of this idea. It describes how much your money can actually buy. If you earn $50 today, that money might cover a trip to the grocery store. But if prices rise and you earn the same $50 next year, you may not be able to buy as many items with it. The purchasing power of your money has dropped, even though the number itself hasn't changed.

Inflation usually happens slowly, year by year, and in many countries it is expected and even considered normal. A little inflation can be a sign of a healthy economy, because it often means people are spending, businesses are growing, and wages rise over time to match higher prices. But too much inflation, or inflation that rises faster than wages, can cause serious problems. When rent, food, or gas prices rise quickly, people feel like their money is slipping through their fingers, even if they are working just as hard as before.

There's also the opposite situation, called deflation, when prices go down. At first, deflation might sound like a good thing. Who wouldn't want cheaper prices? But if it continues for long, it can hurt the economy. Businesses make less money, workers may lose jobs, and people may put off spending because they expect prices to fall even more. That slows down growth and makes recovery difficult.

For you personally, the most important thing to understand is that the value of money is not fixed. Holding on to cash for too long can mean losing purchasing power, because what you can buy with that same amount of money will shrink over time. That's one reason saving in a bank account, investing, or finding other ways to grow your money is so important. Even a small amount of inflation can eat away at your savings if you just let it sit under a mattress.

In everyday life, inflation explains why your rent might go up each year, why groceries slowly get more expensive, or why your paycheck doesn't seem to stretch as far as it used to. Understanding this concept helps you make smarter financial choices. It reminds you that money is not just about the number you see, but what that number can actually get you in the real world.

Interest: Simple vs Compound

Interest is one of the most important concepts in personal finance, because it affects both saving and borrowing. At its core, interest is the cost of using someone else's money, or the reward for letting someone else use yours. When you borrow money, you pay interest. When you save or invest money, you can earn interest.

Simple interest is the easier type to understand. Imagine you borrow $1,000 with a simple interest rate of 5% per year. Each year, you would owe $50 in interest. After three years, you would owe $150 in total interest, plus the $1,000 you originally borrowed. The calculation is straightforward: it's always based on the original amount, also called the principal.

Compound interest, however, works differentl, and it's often called "interest on interest." Instead of being calculated only on the original amount, compound interest is calculated on both the principal and any interest that has already been added. Using the same $1,000 at 5% per year, in the first year you would earn $50, bringing your total to $1,050. In the second year, the 5% is applied to $1,050, not just the original $1,000, so you earn $52.50. By the third year, you earn $55.13, and so on. Over time, the growth speeds up, because each year's interest gets added to the pile and begins earning its own interest.

This difference might not seem huge at first, but over long periods, compound interest can create a massive gap. With simple interest, your money grows in a straight line. With compound interest, your money grows in a curve that gets steeper as time goes on. That's why Albert Einstein supposedly called compound interest the "eighth wonder of the world", because it can turn small amounts into large ones if given enough time.

Of course, compound interest works both ways. It can help you if you are saving or investing, but it can hurt you if you are borrowing. Credit cards, for example, often charge compound interest on balances you don't pay off. That means debt can snowball quickly if you're not careful. On the other hand, investing early, even with small amounts, allows you to take advantage of compounding in a positive way.

Understanding interest helps you see the hidden costs and benefits in financial decisions. When you borrow, you're paying tomorrow for money you use today. When you save or invest, you're letting your money work for you, and the sooner you start, the harder it works.

2.

Budgeting & Managing Personal Finances

Income vs Expenses

The very first step in managing your money is understanding the balance between income and expenses. Income is all the money that comes in. For most young adults, this usually means a paycheck from a job, but income can also come from side hustles, freelance work, tips, government support, or even gifts. It doesn't matter where it comes from. If it puts money in your hands, it's income.

Expenses are the opposite: they're all the things that take money out of your hands. Rent, groceries, transportation, phone bills, streaming services, and the occasional night out with friends are all expenses. Even small things, like grabbing a coffee or paying for parking, count.

The relationship between income and expenses is what determines whether you are moving forward financially or falling behind. If your income is higher than your expenses, you have money left over at the end of the month. That leftover money can be saved, invested, or used for future goals. If your expenses are higher than your income, you are living in the red, which usually leads to borrowing, credit card debt, and stress.

The challenge is that expenses tend to quietly grow. It's easy to sign up for subscriptions you barely use or spend money on conveniences that don't seem like much in the moment but add up over time. On the other hand, increasing income usually takes more effort, like asking for a raise, picking up extra work, or building new skills. That's why most people focus on controlling expenses first: it's the area where you have the most immediate control.

Being aware of your personal balance between income and expenses is the foundation of financial stability. It's like checking the fuel gauge in your car: you need to know whether you're filling up or running on empty. Once you get clear about how much is coming in and how much is going out, you can start making smart decisions about how to manage the difference.

Needs vs Wants

One of the simplest but most powerful ideas in personal finance is learning the difference between needs and wants. A need is something you must have in order to live and function. Food, rent, electricity, basic clothing, and transportation to get to work or school all fall into this category. Without them, life quickly becomes very difficult.

A want, on the other hand, is something that improves your life but isn't necessary for survival. Eating out at restaurants, buying the latest phone, upgrading your wardrobe every season, or subscribing to multiple streaming services are all wants. They make life more enjoyable, but you could live without them if you had to.

The tricky part is that wants often disguise themselves as needs. For example, you absolutely need to eat, but you don't need to order takeout three times a week. You need clothing, but you don't need to buy designer brands. You may need a phone to stay connected, but you don't need the newest model every year. Marketers spend billions of dollars trying to blur this line, convincing you that wants are really needs. Recognizing this trick is half the battle.

Separating needs from wants doesn't mean you should never spend money on things you enjoy. Life isn't meant to be only about survival. But if you spend too much on wants before covering your needs, you'll always feel short on money, no matter how much you earn. The smart approach is to prioritize needs first, then see how much is left over for wants.

Understanding this difference gives you control. Instead of wondering where your money went at the end of the month, you'll know how much you chose to spend on needs and how much you decided to spend on wants. That clarity makes it easier to cut back when necessary and to enjoy your wants without guilt when you can afford them.

How to Create and Stick to a Budget

A budget is simply a plan for your money. It's not about restricting yourself; it's about telling your money where to go instead of wondering where it disappeared. Many people avoid budgeting because they think it's complicated or boring, but at its heart, a budget is just a list of what comes in and what goes out.

The first step in creating a budget is to figure out your income. Write down how much money you actually take home after taxes and deductions. If you work different shifts or freelance, use an average from the last few months to get a realistic picture.

The second step is to track your expenses. This means everything: rent, groceries, bills, transportation, entertainment, subscriptions, and even small daily purchases like coffee. Many people are surprised when they add it all up, because they realize how much disappears on small, forgettable things. Tracking can be done with a notebook, a spreadsheet, or a free app on your phone. The method doesn't matter as much as being honest and consistent.

Once you know your income and expenses, compare them. If your expenses are higher than your income, you need to cut back, starting with wants rather than needs. If you have money left over, you can decide how to use it: saving, investing, or paying off debt are usually the smartest moves.

A common method that many beginners find useful is the 50/30/20 rule. It suggests spending about 50% of your income on needs, 30% on wants, and 20% on savings or paying off debt. It's not a strict law, but it gives you a starting point. If your rent is high or your income is small, your percentages may look different, but the important thing is that you're intentional about it.

Sticking to a budget is often the hardest part. Life is full of temptations and surprises. The key is to make your budget realistic. If it's too strict, you'll give up quickly. Allow yourself some flexibility for fun, but keep it within limits. Checking your budget regularly (weekly or monthly) helps keep you on track. Over time, it becomes a habit, and instead of feeling like a burden, it feels like a safety net.

Budgeting gives you control and peace of mind. Instead of living paycheck to paycheck and hoping things work out, you'll know exactly where you stand. That knowledge makes it easier to reach your goals, avoid debt, and reduce stress about money.

Emergency Funds

Life is full of surprises, and not all of them are pleasant. Cars break down, people lose jobs, medical bills show up, or unexpected expenses appear at the worst possible time. An emergency fund is money set aside specifically for these situations. It acts like a financial safety net so that when life throws you a curveball, you don't have to go into debt just to handle it.

The idea is simple: put money into a separate savings account and don't touch it unless it's a real emergency. A "real emergency" means something necessary and unexpected, not concert tickets, not a sale at your favorite store, and not a vacation. It's for situations where you truly need money right away to cover essentials.

How much should you save? A common rule of thumb is to aim for at least three months' worth of living expenses, and ideally six. That means if your rent, bills, food, and other basic needs cost you $2,000 a month, your emergency fund goal would be $6,000 to $12,000. That may sound like a lot, but you don't need to reach it overnight. Even a few hundred dollars set aside can make a huge difference when something unexpected happens.

The best way to build an emergency fund is little by little. Set aside a small portion of each paycheck, even if it's only $20 or $50 at first. Treat it like a bill you owe yourself. Over time, those small amounts add up. The key is consistency and keeping the money separate so you aren't tempted to dip into it for everyday spending.

Having an emergency fund gives you more than just financial stability. It gives you peace of mind. You'll worry less about "what if" scenarios, because you'll know you have a cushion. That confidence makes it easier to take smart risks, plan for the future, and stay out of the debt cycle when life doesn't go as planned.

3.

Taxes Made Simple

Why Taxes Exist

Taxes are one of those things almost everyone complains about, but they are also one of the main reasons modern life works the way it does. At the most basic level, taxes are money collected by the government to pay for public goods and services. Every time you drive on a road, attend a public school, call the fire department, or walk in a city park, you are using something that taxes helped pay for.

In the past, before modern tax systems, governments often relied on inconsistent or unfair methods to raise money, like demanding goods directly from farmers or taking resources by force. Today, taxes are more structured. Citizens contribute money, and in return, governments provide services, protection, and infrastructure that individuals could never build on their own.

Think about it this way: no single person could afford to build a highway, a hospital, or an entire school system. But when millions of people each contribute a small portion of their income, those resources become possible. Taxes also fund important safety nets, such as unemployment benefits, healthcare programs, or retirement pensions, depending on where you live.

Of course, taxes are never perfect. People often debate whether governments spend tax money wisely, or whether the tax system is fair. These debates will probably never end, because people have different opinions about what is most important. But regardless of politics, taxes exist because societies need a way to pool resources so everyone benefits.

In short, taxes are the price we pay for living in an organized community. They keep the lights on, the streets paved, and the systems running that we often take for granted.

Different Types of Taxes

Taxes come in many forms, and understanding the main ones helps you make sense of where your money goes. Even if you don't notice them directly, most people pay several kinds of taxes throughout their lives.

The most familiar is income tax. This is the portion of money you pay on what you earn from a job, freelance work, or investments. Governments usually collect income tax automatically from your paycheck before you even see the money, which is why the amount you take home is less than what your employer says you earn.

Another common type is sales tax, or value-added tax (VAT). This is paid whenever you buy goods or services. It's usually included as a percentage added to the price at checkout. For example, if you buy a shirt for $20 and the sales tax is 10%, you'll actually pay $22. You might not feel sales tax as much as income tax, but it adds up over time because you pay it almost every day when you shop.

Property tax is another important one, though it only applies if you own real estate. Homeowners pay a percentage of their property's value each year to the local government. This money often goes directly into funding schools, police, fire departments, and other local services. Renters don't pay property tax directly, but landlords usually factor it into rent prices.

Then there's capital gains tax, which applies when you make money from selling something valuable, like stocks, real estate, or even collectibles. For example, if you buy a stock for $1,000 and later sell it for $1,500, the $500 profit may be taxed as a capital gain. This type of tax matters more once you start investing or owning assets.

Beyond these, there are many other smaller taxes that vary by country: inheritance taxes, fuel taxes, luxury taxes, and more. You don't need to memorize them all, but it's useful to recognize that taxes don't just come out of your paycheck. They appear in many parts of life, sometimes in ways that are easy to overlook.

How to Read a Payslip

When you start your first job, one of the first confusing pieces of paper (or online document) you'll see is your payslip. A payslip shows how much money you earned and where it went before it reached your bank account. Understanding it is important, because it helps you see exactly how taxes and other deductions affect your income.

At the top of the payslip, you'll usually find your gross income. This is the total amount you earned before anything was taken out. It might include your regular wages or salary, overtime pay, and bonuses. Many people are surprised to learn that their gross income is higher than the amount that actually shows up in their bank account.

Next come the deductions. These are amounts taken out of your paycheck for different purposes. The biggest one is usually income tax. Depending on your country, you may also see deductions for social security, healthcare, retirement contributions, or other government programs. Some deductions are mandatory, while others are optional, such as contributions to a workplace pension or health insurance plan.

After all the deductions, what remains is your net income, often called "take-home pay." This is the money you actually get to spend or save. It's the number that really matters for budgeting, because it represents your real financial position.

Payslips may also include information like how many hours you worked, your hourly rate (if applicable), and your year-to-date totals, which show how much you've earned and paid in taxes since the beginning of the year.

The first time you look at a payslip, it can feel like half your money has vanished. But once you understand the breakdown, it becomes clearer that part of your earnings is being set aside for taxes, benefits, and future security. Learning to read your payslip gives you a realistic picture of your income and helps you avoid surprises at tax time.

Basics of Filing Taxes

Filing taxes is the process of officially reporting your income and deductions to the government each year. Even though taxes are often taken out of your paycheck automatically, filing is how you make sure the right amount was paid: not too little, not too much.

When you file, you usually fill out a form (on paper or online) that lists how much money you earned, how much tax was already withheld from your paychecks, and whether you qualify for any deductions or credits. Deductions are expenses that reduce the amount of income you are taxed on, such as student loan interest or certain work-related costs. Credits directly reduce the amount of tax you owe, and sometimes they can even give you money back.

After everything is added up, one of two things happens. If too much tax was taken out of your paycheck during the year, you get a refund. This is why many people look forward to tax season: it feels like free money, even though it's really just the government returning what you overpaid. If too little was taken out, you may owe additional taxes, which means you have to send money to the government to cover the difference.

In many countries, there are free or low-cost ways to file taxes, especially if your income is simple and straightforward. If your finances are more complicated, for example, if you're self-employed, own property, or have multiple sources of income, you might use tax software or hire a professional.

The key is not to ignore taxes. Filing late or failing to file at all can lead to penalties, fees, or legal trouble. The good news is that once you've done it once or twice, it stops feeling so intimidating. The more you understand how filing works, the easier it becomes to keep your finances in order year after year.

4.

Banking & Financial Tools

How Bank Accounts Work (Checking/ Savings)

A bank account is one of the most basic financial tools you'll ever use. At its core, it's simply a safe place to store your money, but it also gives you access to services that make everyday life easier. Instead of keeping cash under your mattress, a bank account protects your money, helps you manage it, and connects you to the larger financial system.

There are two main types of accounts most people use: checking accounts and savings accounts. A checking account is designed for everyday spending. This is where your paycheck usually gets deposited and where you pay bills, use your debit card, or withdraw cash. Checking accounts are flexible, but they usually don't earn much, if any, interest. They're more about access than growth.

A savings account, on the other hand, is designed for holding money you don't need to spend right away. It pays interest, which means the bank gives you a small percentage of your balance as a reward for keeping your money there. The interest is usually modest, but it's better than nothing, and savings accounts are great for building up reserves for future goals or emergencies.

Behind the scenes, when you put money in the bank, it doesn't just sit there untouched. Banks use deposits to make loans to other people or businesses, and in return, they give you access to your money whenever you need it. This system works because not everyone needs their money at the same time. That's also why banks can afford to pay you interest, even if it's small.

For most young adults, opening both a checking account and a savings account is the first step into the financial world. Keeping your daily spending money and your savings separate makes it easier to avoid overspending and helps you get into the habit of saving regularly. Over time, as your finances grow, these accounts form the foundation for more advanced tools like investments, retirement accounts, or credit.

Debit vs Credit Cards

Debit cards and credit cards may look almost identical, but they work in very different ways. Knowing the difference is crucial, because how you use them can affect not only your day-to-day finances but also your long-term financial health.

A debit card is directly linked to your checking account. When you swipe it at a store or use it online, the money comes straight out of your account, just like handing over cash. This makes debit cards simple and safe for everyday spending, since you can't spend more than what you actually have. If there's only $200 in your account, you can't buy something for $300, since the transaction will usually be declined. Using a debit card is a good way to avoid debt, but it doesn't help you build credit history, which is something you'll eventually need for bigger financial steps like renting an apartment or buying a car.

A credit card, on the other hand, is more like a short-term loan from the bank. When you use it, you're not spending your own money right away; you're borrowing money with the promise to pay it back later. If you pay off the balance in full each month, a credit card works smoothly, almost like a debit card, but with extra perks like rewards points, purchase protection, or cashback. The risk comes if you don't pay the balance in full. Unpaid amounts carry over to the next month, and the bank charges interest, often at very high rates. That's how small purchases can turn into large debts if you're not careful.

The biggest difference between debit and credit is their effect on your financial future. Debit cards help you manage your own money, but they don't build your credit score. Credit cards, if used wisely, can help establish a strong credit history, showing lenders that you can borrow and repay responsibly. That history matters when applying for loans, mortgages, or even jobs in some industries.

The best approach is balance. Use your debit card for everyday expenses to stay grounded in what you actually have, and use a credit card for controlled purchases that you can pay off in full each month. This way, you avoid debt while still building the credit history you'll need later in life.

Loans, Mortgages, and Interest Rates Explained

At some point in life, most people borrow money. It might be for college, buying a car, starting a business, or purchasing a home. Borrowing can feel overwhelming at first, but at its core, a loan is simply an agreement: you get money now and promise to pay it back later, usually with interest.

A loan works like this: the lender (a bank or financial institution) gives you a certain amount of money. You agree to repay it over time, often in monthly installments. But because the lender is taking on risk and providing you money upfront, they charge interest: an extra percentage added to what you owe. This interest is how the lender makes money and ensures they're compensated for the risk of lending.

Mortgages are just a special type of loan, usually the largest one you'll ever take. They are specifically for buying a home and can last 15, 20, or even 30 years. Because the loan is so big, the home itself serves as collateral. That means if you stop paying, the bank can take the house back. While that sounds scary, mortgages allow ordinary people to afford houses without needing all the money upfront.

Interest rates are what really determine how expensive a loan becomes. A small difference in rates can make a huge impact over time. For example, if you borrow $10,000 at 5% interest, you'll pay far less in the long run than if you borrow the same amount at 15%. That's why shopping around for the best rate is important before taking out any loan. Rates depend on factors like your credit score, the type of loan, and the overall economy.

The golden rule with loans is this: only borrow what you can realistically repay, and always pay attention to the total cost, not just the monthly payment. Sometimes lenders make payments look small by stretching them out over many years, but that usually means you'll pay much more in interest overall.

Used wisely, loans and mortgages can open doors to education, cars, and homes that would otherwise be out of reach. Used recklessly, they can trap you in long-term debt. Understanding how interest works, and being realistic about what you can afford, makes all the difference.

Good Debt vs Bad Debt

Not all debt is created equal. While the word "debt" often sounds negative, some types of borrowing can actually help you move forward in life. The key is understanding the difference between good debt and bad debt.

Good debt is borrowing that has the potential to increase your future wealth or improve your life in meaningful ways. For example, taking out student loans (within reason) can be good debt if it helps you gain education and skills that lead to better job opportunities. A mortgage is another form of good debt, since buying a home can build equity over time instead of just paying rent forever. Even a small business loan can be good debt if it allows you to grow something that generates income. The common thread is that good debt is an investment in your future.

Bad debt, on the other hand, usually comes from borrowing for things that don't grow in value and may even lose value quickly. Credit card debt for clothes, gadgets, or vacations is classic bad debt, especially because the interest rates are so high. A car loan can also slip into bad debt territory if you buy a vehicle far more expensive than you can reasonably afford, since cars lose value the moment they leave the dealership. In short, bad debt takes money out of your future without giving you much in return.

The tricky part is that the same type of debt can be good or bad depending on how it's used. For instance, student loans can be good if they're manageable and lead to a useful degree, but bad if you borrow way more than you can pay back for a program that doesn't improve your career prospects. A credit card can help build your credit score if paid off each month, but it becomes bad debt if balances spiral out of control.

The rule of thumb is this: good debt helps you build assets, skills, or opportunities; bad debt drains your resources without lasting benefit. If you keep this distinction in mind, you'll be able to make smarter borrowing decisions and avoid traps that keep many people stuck in financial stress.

5.

Insurance: Protecting Yourself

Why Insurance Matters

Life is full of uncertainty. No matter how careful you are, accidents, illnesses, or unexpected events can happen. Insurance exists to protect you from the financial impact of those situations. Instead of facing huge costs on your own, you pay a smaller, regular amount to an insurance company, and in return, they step in to cover big expenses if something goes wrong.

Think of insurance like a safety net. For example, imagine you get into a car accident that causes $20,000 worth of damage. Very few people have that kind of money lying around. But if you have auto insurance, the company helps pay the costs, so you're not financially ruined by one bad day. Similarly, health insurance helps with medical bills, which can be extremely high even for minor issues. Home insurance protects your house and belongings from disasters like fires or theft. Life insurance provides money for your family if you pass away, helping them stay financially stable.

Insurance works because lots of people contribute a little money, and only some need big payouts at any given time. This pooling of risk spreads the cost so no single person has to carry it alone. Without insurance, one unexpected event could wipe out years of savings and leave you struggling for decades.

Some people see insurance as a waste because you may never "use it." But the truth is, insurance is not about small wins. It's about avoiding massive losses. The peace of mind it brings is valuable on its own, and in many cases, certain types of insurance (like auto or health) are legally required.

In short, insurance matters because it protects your finances, your future, and the people who depend on you. It won't stop bad things from happening, but it makes sure one accident or illness doesn't destroy your entire financial foundation.

Health, Auto, Home, Life Insurance Basics

There are many types of insurance, but four of the most common and important are health, auto, home, and life insurance. Each serves a different purpose, and together they cover many of the biggest risks you might face.

Health Insurance:

Health care can be extremely expensive. Even a short hospital stay or a simple surgery can cost thousands of dollars. Health insurance helps cover these costs so you don't have to pay the full amount out of pocket. Depending on your plan, it may cover doctor visits, prescriptions, emergency care, and preventive services like check-ups or vaccines. In many countries, health insurance is either required or heavily encouraged, because medical costs without it can be overwhelming.

Auto Insurance:

If you drive, auto insurance is almost always a legal requirement. It protects you financially if you're in a car accident. This includes covering damage to your own car, the other person's car, medical bills if someone gets hurt, and sometimes even theft or natural disasters. Since accidents are so common and expensive, auto insurance is considered essential for any driver.

Home Insurance:

Homeowners insurance protects your house and belongings against risks like fire, theft, or natural disasters. If something happens, the insurance company helps pay for repairs or replacements. Even if you don't own a home, renters insurance is often recommended. It's usually cheap and covers your personal belongings in case of theft, water damage, or other unexpected events.

Life Insurance:

Life insurance is a bit different. It doesn't protect you directly but instead protects your loved ones if you pass away. The insurance company pays out a lump sum to the people you choose (your beneficiaries), which can help them pay for living expenses, debts, or even future goals like education. This type of insurance is especially important if you have dependents who rely on your income.

Each of these insurances focuses on a specific area of life, but together they provide a safety net for many of the most common risks. The goal isn't to cover every possible problem but to protect against the ones that could do the most financial damage.

How Premiums, Deductibles, and Coverage Work

Insurance comes with its own set of terms that can feel confusing at first, but once you understand them, the whole system makes a lot more sense. The three most important words you'll hear are premium, deductible, and coverage.

The premium is the price you pay to keep your insurance active. Think of it as a subscription fee. You might pay it monthly, every six months, or once a year. For example, if your car insurance premium is $100 per month, that's the cost of maintaining your protection even if you don't file a claim.

The deductible is the amount you agree to pay out of pocket before the insurance company starts helping. Let's say your health insurance has a $500 deductible, and you end up with a $2,000 hospital bill. You pay the first $500, and the insurance covers the rest (depending on your policy). Deductibles exist so that you share some responsibility, which helps keep premiums from being sky-high.

Coverage is what the insurance actually protects you against, and up to what limit. For example, your auto insurance might cover accidents, theft, and storm damage, but not routine maintenance like oil changes. Coverage also has limits: the maximum amount the company will pay. If your home insurance policy covers fire damage up to $200,000 and your house costs $300,000 to rebuild, you'd have to pay the difference.

Here's how they all work together: if you want lower premiums, you might choose a plan with a higher deductible. If you'd rather not risk paying much out of pocket during an emergency, you'd choose a lower deductible, but that usually means a higher premium. Coverage ensures you know what situations you're actually protected from, so reading the fine print is essential.

In short: premiums are what you pay regularly, deductibles are what you pay when something happens, and coverage defines what the insurance company pays for. Understanding this trio is the key to knowing what kind of protection you really have.

Avoiding Overpaying for Insurance

Insurance is important, but it's also easy to end up paying more than you need to. Companies often offer lots of add-ons and extras that sound nice but don't actually give you much value. The key is to find the right balance: enough coverage to protect you from real risks, but not so much that you're wasting money.

One common mistake is buying duplicate coverage. For example, if you already have good health insurance, you probably don't need extra "accident insurance" that overlaps with it. Or if you're renting an apartment, you don't need the same level of home insurance as someone who owns a house. Always check whether your existing policies already cover certain risks before signing up for more.

Another tip is to shop around. Different companies can charge very different premiums for almost identical coverage. Spending an hour comparing quotes could save you hundreds of dollars a year. Also, review your policies regularly. As your life changes (maybe you pay off a car loan, move to a safer neighborhood, or buy fewer valuables) your insurance needs may shrink, and your premiums should go down too.

Deductibles are another way to save. If you can afford to cover small emergencies yourself, choosing a higher deductible often lowers your premium. Just make sure you actually have the money set aside in case something happens.

Finally, be wary of emotional sales pitches. Insurance companies often try to sell you peace of mind by adding on coverage you'll likely never use. It's smart to protect yourself, but remember that insurance is about financial security, not buying every possible safeguard.

In short, the best way to avoid overpaying is to know what you really need, compare options, and update your policies as your situation changes. That way, you stay protected without throwing money away.

6.

Investing 101

Difference Between Saving and Investing

Saving and investing might seem similar (after all, both involve putting money aside for the future), but they serve very different purposes and work in very different ways. Understanding the difference is one of the most important steps toward building real financial security.

Saving is about safety and short-term goals. When you save, you typically keep your money in a place that's low-risk and easy to access, like a savings account. The goal is to protect your money and have it ready when you need it: whether that's for an emergency, a vacation, or a new laptop. Because it's low-risk, savings don't grow much beyond what you put in. Interest rates on savings accounts are usually small, so while your money is safe, it doesn't grow quickly.

Investing, on the other hand, is about growth and long-term goals. When you invest, you use your money to buy assets like stocks, bonds, or funds that have the potential to increase in value over time. The trade-off is risk: the value of your investments can go up or down, and there's no guarantee of returns. However, because of that risk, investing offers the chance for much higher growth compared to saving, which is why it's the main way people build wealth over decades.

The key difference is time and purpose. Saving is best for short-term needs (like emergencies or near-future purchases) and for money you can't afford to lose. Investing is best for long-term goals (like retirement or buying a home in 10+ years), where you can handle the ups and downs of the market because you're not depending on the money right away.

In reality, a healthy financial plan includes both. You save to protect yourself and stay prepared for the unexpected, and you invest to make your money work for you and grow over time. Understanding how to balance the two is one of the most important financial skills you can learn.

Stocks, Bonds, Funds, ETFs

When people talk about investing, you'll often hear terms like stocks, bonds, funds, or ETFs. These are the building blocks of most investment strategies, and while they can sound intimidating, the basics are actually pretty straightforward.

Stocks represent ownership in a company. When you buy a share of stock, you literally own a small piece of that company. If the company grows and makes money, the value of your stock can go up, and you might also receive dividends (a portion of the profits paid to shareholders). Stocks can grow a lot in value over time, but they can also drop suddenly, which makes them riskier in the short term.

Bonds are basically loans. When you buy a bond, you're lending money to a government or a company, and in return, they agree to pay you interest over time and give your original money back later. Bonds are usually safer than stocks, but they also tend to grow more slowly. They're often used to balance out the risk in an investment portfolio.

Funds are collections of many different investments grouped together. Instead of buying just one stock or one bond, you can buy into a fund that owns hundreds or even thousands of them. This makes investing easier and safer because your risk is spread out. Mutual funds, for example, are managed by professionals who choose which investments to include.

ETFs (Exchange-Traded Funds) are a lot like mutual funds, but they trade on the stock market like individual stocks. This means you can buy or sell them throughout the day, often with lower fees. Many ETFs simply track an index, like the S&P 500, which represents the performance of the biggest companies in the U.S.

Here's the simple takeaway:

- Stocks = ownership in companies, higher risk, higher potential reward.
- Bonds = loans to companies/governments, lower risk, lower reward.
- Funds/ETFs = bundles of many stocks and/or bonds, giving you diversification and balance.

Most successful investors don't put all their money into just one stock or bond. Instead, they use funds or ETFs to spread out risk while still benefiting from long-term growth.

Retirement Accounts (401k, IRA, Pensions, Depending on Region)

Retirement accounts are special tools designed to help you save and invest for the time when you stop working. Unlike a regular savings or investment account, these accounts often come with tax benefits or employer contributions that make your money grow faster. The details vary by country, but the idea is the same: governments encourage people to save for retirement by offering extra perks.

In the United States, the two most common types are the 401(k) and the IRA. A 401(k) is offered by many employers. You can choose to have part of your paycheck automatically go into this account, and sometimes your employer will even match a portion of your contributions, which is essentially free money. An IRA (Individual Retirement Account) is something you open on your own if your employer doesn't offer a 401(k), or if you want to save more beyond it. Both accounts allow your investments to grow with tax advantages, meaning you either don't pay taxes until later or you avoid them on your growth altogether, depending on the type.

In other regions, the names and systems may differ, but the purpose is the same. In the UK, there are workplace pensions and personal pensions. In Canada, there's the RRSP (Registered Retirement Savings Plan). In many countries, there's also some form of government pension or social security that provides a basic income in retirement, but it's rarely enough to cover everything, so private saving is important.

The main thing to remember is that retirement accounts are designed for the long term. Taking money out early often comes with penalties and taxes, which is why they're best left untouched until retirement age.

The benefit is that by starting early, even small amounts can grow into large sums thanks to compound interest and decades of investment growth.

The takeaway is simple: if you have access to a retirement account, start contributing as soon as possible, even if it's just a small percentage of your paycheck. The earlier you begin, the less you'll need to save later, because time does most of the heavy lifting for you.

The Power of Long-Term Investing

When it comes to investing, time is your greatest ally. Markets go up and down in the short term, sometimes dramatically, but over the long term they have historically trended upward. The secret to building wealth isn't trying to predict every rise and fall. It's staying invested long enough to let growth and compound interest work for you.

Imagine you invest $1,000 and it grows by just 7% per year (a common long-term average for stock markets). After one year, you'll have $1,070. That doesn't sound like much. But if you leave it invested, the next year you earn interest not just on your original $1,000, but on the $1,070. Over decades, this snowball effect becomes powerful. That same $1,000 could grow to nearly $8,000 in 40 years without you adding another cent. If you keep adding money along the way, the growth is even more dramatic.

The flip side is that people who jump in and out of the market, chasing quick profits, often lose money. Timing the market is extremely difficult, even for professionals. Long-term investing isn't about getting rich overnight; it's about building wealth steadily over time. The earlier you start, the more time your money has to grow, which is why young adults have such an advantage.

Patience is the key. Market downturns will happen (sometimes painfully so) but history shows that markets recover and grow over time. Those who stay invested through the ups and downs are usually the ones who come out ahead.

In short, long-term investing turns small, consistent contributions into large future rewards. It's less about being clever and more about being consistent and patient. Start early, keep investing, and let time do the heavy lifting.

7.

Credit & Debt Management

What a Credit Score Is and Why It Matters

Your credit score is like a financial report card. It's a three-digit number, usually ranging from about 300 to 850, that shows how trustworthy you are when it comes to borrowing and repaying money. Lenders, landlords, and even some employers look at your credit score to decide whether they can rely on you.

A high credit score tells lenders that you're responsible with money: you borrow and repay on time. A low score suggests you might be risky to lend to, either because of missed payments, too much debt, or no credit history at all.

Here's why it matters: your credit score can affect almost every major step in your financial life. If you want to rent an apartment, your landlord might check it. If you apply for a car loan or mortgage, it affects not just whether you're approved but also what interest rate you'll pay. A good score can save you thousands of dollars over time because lenders offer lower rates to people they trust.

Your score is usually based on a few main factors:

- Payment history: do you pay your bills on time?
- Credit utilization: how much of your available credit are you using?
- Length of credit history: how long have you had credit accounts open?
- Types of credit: do you have a healthy mix (like a credit card, student loan, etc.)?
- New credit inquiries: how often are you applying for new

accounts?

In simple terms: pay your bills on time, don't max out your credit cards, and keep accounts open for as long as possible. Over time, those habits will naturally raise your score.

A good credit score isn't about bragging rights. It's about access. It gives you more opportunities, better deals, and financial breathing room. That's why understanding and managing it is so important.

How to Build Good Credit

Building good credit isn't complicated, but it does take time and consistent habits. Think of it like building a reputation: you can't do it overnight, but steady, responsible behavior will create a strong record that works in your favor.

The most important step is to pay all your bills on time. Even one late payment can hurt your credit score, and the longer it takes you to catch up, the worse the damage. Setting up automatic payments or reminders can help you stay on track.

Next, try to keep your credit utilization low. This means not maxing out your credit cards. A good rule of thumb is to use less than 30% of your available credit. For example, if your card limit is $1,000, try not to carry a balance higher than $300. Lenders see lower utilization as a sign that you manage debt responsibly.

Start small if you're new to credit. If you don't qualify for a regular credit card, you can begin with a secured card (where you put down a deposit as collateral) or become an authorized user on a family member's card. Using these responsibly builds your history over time.

It also helps to keep accounts open for the long term. The longer your credit history, the better your score looks. Closing old accounts can shorten your history and may hurt your score, so think carefully before canceling cards, especially your oldest ones.

Finally, don't apply for too much credit at once. Each application can cause a small dip in your score, and too many applications in a short period may make you look desperate for credit. Apply only when you really need to.

The formula for building credit is simple: borrow a little, pay it back reliably, and repeat. Over time, these good habits create a track record that lenders trust, which translates to better opportunities, lower interest rates, and more financial freedom.

Dangers of High-Interest Debt (Credit Cards, Payday Loans)

Not all debt is the same, and some kinds can drag you down faster than you expect. The most dangerous debt is high-interest debt, because it grows quickly and can trap you in a cycle that's hard to escape. Two of the most common examples are credit card balances and payday loans.

Credit cards can be useful tools when used wisely, but the interest rates are usually very high: often 15%, 20%, or even more. If you carry a balance instead of paying your card off in full each month, the interest adds up quickly. For example, if you owe $1,000 and only make minimum payments, you could end up paying hundreds of extra dollars in interest and take years to get rid of the debt. Small purchases can snowball into huge burdens if left unpaid.

Payday loans are even worse. These are short-term loans meant to "tide you over" until your next paycheck. They often come with sky-high fees and interest rates that can exceed 300% per year. What looks like a quick solution to a money problem can quickly spiral into a debt trap, with borrowers needing to take out new loans just to pay off the old ones.

The danger of high-interest debt is that it eats away at your income. Instead of your money going toward things you want or need, it goes toward paying interest. This makes it harder to save, invest, or get ahead financially. It's like running on a treadmill: you're working hard but not really moving forward.

The best defense is to avoid high-interest debt whenever possible. Pay off credit card balances in full each month, and steer clear of payday loans altogether. If you find yourself stuck in high-interest debt, tackling it should become a top priority before focusing on other financial goals.

High-interest debt is like quicksand: easy to fall into, but very hard to climb out of. Recognizing the risks is the first step to staying safe.

Strategies for Paying Off Debt

Getting out of debt might feel overwhelming, but with the right strategies, it's completely doable. The key is to make a plan, stick to it, and build momentum as you go.

One popular method is the debt snowball. With this approach, you focus on paying off your smallest debt first while making minimum payments on the others. Once that smallest debt is gone, you move on to the next smallest, and so on. Each payoff gives you a psychological win, which motivates you to keep going until you're debt-free.

Another option is the debt avalanche. Here, you focus on the debt with the highest interest rate first, while still making minimum payments on the rest. Mathematically, this saves you the most money in interest over time. It may take longer to see the first balance disappear compared to the snowball method, but it's the most cost-effective strategy.

For some people, a mix of both works best: maybe starting with one small balance for the motivation, then switching to the highest-interest debt afterward.

Beyond these methods, you can also look into consolidating debt. This means combining multiple debts into one, ideally at a lower interest rate. Options include balance transfer credit cards (with 0% introductory offers) or personal loans. Just be careful not to rack up new debt while consolidating the old.

Other helpful steps include:

- Cutting unnecessary expenses and directing that money toward your debt.

- Increasing your income, even temporarily, with side gigs or extra hours, to speed up repayment.
- Automating payments so you don't miss due dates and rack up late fees.

Paying off debt isn't just about money; it's about freedom. Every payment gets you closer to having your income fully belong to you again. Stick with the plan, stay consistent, and the weight of debt will eventually lift.

8.

Housing & Renting vs Owning

Renting: Leases, Deposits, Tenants' Rights

For many young adults, renting is the first step toward independent living. It's usually more flexible and affordable than buying a home, but it comes with its own rules and responsibilities.

When you rent, you typically sign a lease, which is a legal contract between you and the landlord. The lease spells out the rent amount, how long you'll stay (commonly 12 months), and rules such as whether pets are allowed or who pays for utilities. Always read the lease carefully before signing, since it's a binding agreement.

Most landlords also require a security deposit, usually equal to one or two months' rent. This is money held by the landlord in case you damage the property or leave owing rent. If you take care of the place and pay on time, you usually get the deposit back when you move out.

As a tenant, you also have rights. While the details vary by country or state, common rights include:

- The right to a safe and habitable home (no serious leaks, mold, or broken heating).
- Protection from unfair eviction (a landlord can't just throw you out without notice).
- The right to privacy (landlords usually must give notice before entering your home).

On the flip side, you have responsibilities too, like paying rent on time, keeping the place reasonably clean, and not causing damage beyond normal wear and tear.

Renting can be a great option if you value flexibility, don't want to deal with maintenance, or aren't ready to settle in one place. Just remember: your lease is a contract, deposits aren't "free money," and knowing your rights can save you from being taken advantage of.

Buying a House: Mortgages, Down Payments, Property Taxes

Buying a home is often described as one of the biggest financial decisions in life. Unlike renting, where you pay for the right to live somewhere temporarily, buying means you're building ownership over time. But it also comes with big responsibilities and long-term commitments.

Most people don't have enough money to buy a house outright, which is why they take out a mortgage. A mortgage is a special kind of loan used to buy property. You borrow money from a bank or lender and pay it back over a long period, often 15 to 30 years, with interest. The home itself acts as collateral, meaning if you don't pay, the bank can take it back through foreclosure.

When buying, you usually need to make a down payment, which is the portion of the home's price you pay upfront. The rest is covered by the mortgage. The size of the down payment often affects the mortgage terms. A larger down payment can mean lower monthly payments and sometimes better interest rates, while a very small one can lead to higher costs and the need for extra insurance.

Another ongoing cost of homeownership is property taxes. These are taxes charged by local governments, often based on the value of your home. They help fund things like schools, roads, and emergency services. Property taxes are usually collected annually or semi-annually, though many lenders include them in your monthly mortgage payment so you don't have to pay a big lump sum once a year.

In addition to these, owning a home comes with other costs: maintenance, repairs, insurance, and sometimes association fees. Unlike renting, where the landlord covers most issues, homeowners are responsible for everything from a leaky roof to a broken furnace.

Owning a house can build wealth over time, since you're paying toward something you own rather than paying rent to a landlord. But it's also a long-term financial commitment that requires careful planning and budgeting.

Pros and Cons of Renting vs Owning

Deciding whether to rent or own a home is one of the biggest financial choices you'll make, and the "right" answer depends on your situation. Both options come with benefits and drawbacks.

Renting is usually more flexible. You can move more easily when your lease ends, which is ideal if you're unsure where you want to live long term or if your job might change. Renters don't have to worry about property maintenance or unexpected repair costs, that's the landlord's job. Renting also doesn't require a huge upfront payment like a down payment on a house.

The downside of renting is that your monthly payments don't build ownership. Once you pay rent, that money is gone, and you don't build equity (ownership value in the property). Rent can also rise over time, and you're subject to the landlord's rules.

Owning a home gives you the chance to build equity as you pay off your mortgage. Over time, if your home's value increases, it can also become a valuable asset. Homeownership can provide stability, since you're not at risk of being asked to move when a lease ends. Many people also enjoy the freedom to renovate or customize their own space.

However, owning comes with responsibilities. You're in charge of all repairs, maintenance and insurance, which can get expensive. The upfront costs, like the down payment and closing fees, are much higher than moving into a rental. And unlike renting, selling a house if you want to move can take time and involve extra costs.

In short, renting offers flexibility and lower immediate costs, while owning builds long-term wealth and stability but ties you down with financial and practical commitments. The best choice depends on your stage in life, financial situation, and personal goals.

9.

Work, Paychecks & Employment Basics

Understanding Employment Contracts

When you start a new job, you'll usually be asked to sign an employment contract. This is a written agreement between you and your employer that explains the terms of your work. It's important to understand what you're agreeing to before you sign, because it affects your pay, your rights, and your responsibilities.

An employment contract typically includes details like your job title, salary or hourly wage, working hours, and whether the job is full-time, part-time, or temporary. It also explains expectations. For example, what tasks you're responsible for, who you report to, and rules you're expected to follow.

Some contracts also outline things like probation periods (a trial phase when your employer decides if you're a good fit), non-compete clauses (rules about not working for competitors for a certain time after leaving), or confidentiality agreements (keeping company information private).

It's also worth noting that employment contracts can vary widely depending on the country, region, or type of job. In some places, not all jobs have formal contracts. Instead, workers are employed "at-will," meaning either the employer or employee can end the job at any time, within legal limits.

Before signing, it's always smart to read the contract carefully. If something seems unclear, ask questions. In some cases, you may even be able to negotiate certain terms, such as pay, vacation time, or flexible work arrangements.

Understanding your employment contract helps protect you from surprises later. It's the foundation of your work relationship, so treat it with the same seriousness as any other important agreement in life.

Gross vs Net Income

When you hear people talk about income, it can mean different things depending on whether they're referring to gross or net income. Understanding the difference is key to knowing how much money you actually take home.

Gross income is the total amount of money you earn before anything is taken out. If your job pays you $3,000 a month, that's your gross income. It's the big number you often see listed in your employment contract or job offer.

Net income, often called "take-home pay," is what you actually receive in your bank account after deductions. Deductions can include taxes, social security contributions, health insurance premiums, and retirement plan contributions. So, if your gross monthly income is $3,000, but after all the deductions you only get $2,400, then $2,400 is your net income.

The difference matters because many people make financial plans based on gross income without realizing how much smaller their net income will be. This can lead to budgeting problems if you assume you'll have more money available than you actually do.

In short: gross is what you earn on paper, net is what you can actually spend. Always budget and plan your life around your net income, not the bigger number, so you don't get caught off guard.

Benefits (Healthcare, Retirement Contributions, Vacation)

When you get a job, your pay isn't the only thing that matters. Many employers also offer benefits, which are extra perks or forms of compensation beyond your salary. Benefits can make a big difference in your overall financial health and quality of life.

One of the most important benefits is healthcare. In many countries, especially where healthcare isn't free or fully covered by the government, employers help by providing health insurance. This means the company pays part (sometimes most) of your monthly insurance cost, while you pay the rest. Having employer-sponsored healthcare can save you a lot of money and provide access to better coverage than you might find on your own.

Another common benefit is retirement contributions. Many employers offer retirement plans, such as a 401(k) in the U.S., and some will even match a portion of what you contribute. For example, if you put in 5% of your paycheck, your employer might add another 5%. This is essentially free money toward your future, and taking advantage of it can dramatically boost your long-term savings.

Paid time off (PTO) is also a key benefit. This usually includes vacation days, sick leave, and sometimes personal days. Having paid time off means you can rest, recover, or take care of personal matters without losing income. Some companies are more generous than others, so it's worth paying attention to how much PTO is included in your job offer.

Other benefits may include things like parental leave, professional development allowances, employee discounts, or even flexible working arrangements. While these may not show up in your paycheck, they can add significant value to your overall compensation package.

The bottom line: salary matters, but benefits can make a huge difference in your financial security and work-life balance. Always look at the full package, not just the base pay, when evaluating a job.

Side Hustles & Freelance Income Basics

In today's world, many people don't rely on just one job for their income. Side hustles and freelance work have become common ways to earn extra money, explore passions, or build financial security.

A side hustle is usually a small job or project you do outside of your main job. This could be driving for a rideshare company, selling handmade crafts online, tutoring, or running a small online business. The key is flexibility: side hustles can fit around your regular schedule and provide additional income.

Freelance work is similar, but often more formal and skill-based. Freelancers are self-employed and offer services directly to clients. For example, freelance writers, designers, programmers, or consultants work on projects for different companies or individuals. Freelancers usually set their own rates and schedules, but they're also responsible for managing their own taxes and benefits, since they don't have an employer handling those things.

The benefits of side hustles and freelance income include having extra money to pay off debt, save, or invest. They can also help you build new skills, expand your network, or even turn into a full-time business one day.

However, there are challenges too. Freelance income isn't always steady, and you might have to chase clients for payment. You also need to keep track of your own finances (including setting aside money for taxes) because no employer is automatically deducting them for you.

Whether it's a small side job or a full freelance career, earning outside of traditional employment gives you more control and opportunities.

Just remember that with the freedom comes responsibility: you're your own boss, accountant, and planner.

10.

Entrepreneurship & Small Business Basics

What It Takes to Start a Business

Starting a business is exciting, but it's also challenging. Many people dream of being their own boss, but it's important to understand what goes into making that dream a reality.

The first thing you need is a business idea, something people want or need and are willing to pay for. This could be a product, like baked goods or clothing, or a service, like tutoring or web design. The key is finding a problem you can solve or a value you can provide.

Next comes planning. A good business plan doesn't have to be complicated, but it should outline what you're offering, who your customers are, how you'll reach them, and how much it will cost to run the business. Planning helps you avoid surprises and shows you whether your idea is realistic.

You'll also need some form of funding. Starting costs can include equipment, supplies, marketing, and possibly rent for a space. Some businesses can be started cheaply, while others need significant investment. Funding can come from your savings, loans, or sometimes investors.

Time and effort are just as important as money. Running a business often takes long hours, especially in the beginning. You'll be wearing many hats: manager, marketer, accountant, and customer service representative all at once.

Lastly, you'll need persistence. Not every day will go smoothly, and setbacks are part of the process. Successful entrepreneurs learn from mistakes, adapt, and keep moving forward.

Starting a business isn't easy, but it can be incredibly rewarding. It gives you the chance to create something of your own and potentially achieve financial independence. The key ingredients are a solid idea, a clear plan, enough resources to get going, and the determination to stick with it.

Business Taxes & Registration Basics

When you start a business, it's not just about selling products or services. You also need to handle the legal and financial side. Two of the most important parts are registering your business and understanding business taxes.

Business registration is how you officially set up your company. Depending on your country or region, you may need to choose a legal structure. Common options include:

- Sole proprietorship: the simplest form, where you and the business are the same legally. Easy to start, but you're personally responsible for all debts.
- Partnership: when two or more people run a business together. Profits (and risks) are shared.
- Corporation/limited company (LLC, Ltd, etc.): a separate legal entity that protects your personal assets from business debts, but is more complex and requires more paperwork.

Registering your business usually involves filling out forms with your government, paying a fee, and sometimes getting licenses or permits depending on your industry.

Once you're registered, you'll also need to deal with business taxes. Just like individuals, businesses pay taxes on their income. The type and amount depend on your business structure and where you live. For example, sole proprietors often pay income tax through their personal return, while corporations file separate tax returns.

On top of income tax, businesses may also need to collect sales tax or VAT if they sell goods or services, and they might have to pay payroll taxes if they hire employees. Keeping track of these responsibilities is essential to avoid fines or legal trouble.

Because taxes and rules can be complex, many small business owners work with an accountant or tax professional. Even if your business is small, getting advice early can save you from costly mistakes later.

In short: registering makes your business official, and paying the right taxes keeps it legal. These steps may not be the most exciting part of entrepreneurship, but they're the foundation that allows your business to grow safely.

Profits, Expenses, Reinvestment

One of the most important things to understand in business is the difference between income, expenses, and profit; and what you do with those profits once you earn them.

Income is the money your business brings in from selling products or services. Expenses are the costs of running the business: things like rent, supplies, employee wages, utilities, or advertising.

When you subtract expenses from income, what's left is your profit (sometimes called the "bottom line"). Profit is the reward for running the business, but it's also fuel for growth.

Here's where reinvestment comes in. Instead of taking all the profit out of the business for yourself, smart business owners put some of it back into the company. This could mean upgrading equipment, hiring staff, improving marketing, or developing new products. Reinvesting helps the business grow and increases the chance of earning even more profit in the future.

At the same time, it's important to balance reinvestment with paying yourself. Many small business owners fall into the trap of either taking too much money out (leaving the business underfunded) or taking too little (struggling to cover personal needs). The goal is to find a healthy balance where both you and the business can thrive.

Another key is keeping good financial records. Tracking every expense and income source not only helps you understand whether you're really making money, but also keeps you prepared for taxes and future planning.

In short: income is what comes in, expenses are what goes out, profit is what remains; and reinvestment is how you turn today's success into tomorrow's growth.

Risks and Rewards

Starting and running a business is never risk-free, but the potential rewards can make it worthwhile. Understanding both sides helps you prepare for challenges and stay realistic about what entrepreneurship involves.

The risks include financial loss, since you often need to invest your own money to get started. There's no guarantee customers will buy what you're offering, and many new businesses fail within the first few years. Income can be unpredictable, especially in the beginning, making it harder to budget or plan. You may also face personal stress, long working hours, and the pressure of being responsible for everything: from sales to customer service to paying bills.

On the other hand, the rewards can be life-changing. Owning a business gives you independence and control: you're your own boss, setting your own vision. If your business succeeds, the financial upside can be much greater than a regular paycheck, since profits are yours to keep after expenses. There's also personal satisfaction in building something from scratch, solving problems, and seeing customers value what you've created.

Some entrepreneurs find the risks overwhelming, while others thrive on the challenge. The key is to manage risks by planning carefully, starting small when possible, and being willing to adapt. At the same time, keeping your eye on the potential rewards helps you stay motivated through the difficult parts.

In short: entrepreneurship is a high-risk, high-reward path. It requires resilience, but for those who succeed, the payoff isn't just money. It's freedom, growth, and the pride of creating something of your own.

11.

Consumer Skills & Smart Spending

How Advertising Influences Choices

Every day, we're surrounded by advertising: on TV, online, in stores, and even on social media. Ads are designed to get your attention and influence your decisions, often in ways you don't even notice.

Advertising works by creating desire. Companies want you to believe that their product will make your life better, easier, or more enjoyable. They may use emotional appeals, like showing happy families using their product, or social pressure, like suggesting "everyone" has the latest gadget.

Another common tactic is scarcity and urgency. Ads might say things like "limited-time offer" or "only a few left in stock," pushing you to buy quickly before thinking it through.

Social media has made advertising even more subtle. Influencers often promote products in ways that feel like friendly recommendations, but they're still paid promotions. This blurs the line between genuine advice and marketing.

Understanding these tactics doesn't mean advertising is always bad. Sometimes ads introduce you to products you actually need or enjoy. But it's important to stay aware and ask yourself: *Do I really want this, or am I just being persuaded by clever marketing?*

Being conscious of how advertising works helps you make smarter choices, spend money on what truly matters to you, and avoid buying things just because an ad made it look appealing.

Reading Contracts and Fine Print

Contracts are everywhere, from signing up for a phone plan to renting an apartment, buying a car, or agreeing to online terms of service. A contract is a legally binding agreement, and once you sign, you're responsible for following it. That's why it's important to read carefully, especially the fine print.

The fine print often contains the most important details, but it's written in small text or legal language that people tend to skip. This is where companies put information about extra fees, cancellation policies, penalties, or limitations on what you're actually getting.

For example, a gym membership might look like it's month-to-month, but the fine print could say you're locked in for a full year. A "free trial" might automatically turn into a paid subscription if you don't cancel in time.

When reading a contract, look for:

- Costs: Are there hidden fees or charges?
- Length: How long are you locked in? Can you cancel early?.
- Responsibilities: What are you agreeing to do? What happens if you don't?
- Company's obligations: What are they promising you in return?

If something seems unclear, ask questions or request clarification before signing. Don't be afraid to take time to read the whole thing. Rushing benefits the company, not you.

Remember: once you sign, "I didn't read it" is not an excuse. Being careful with contracts protects your money and keeps you from being trapped in unfair agreements.

Avoiding Scams and Predatory Lending

In today's world, scams and shady lenders are everywhere. They often target people who are young, inexperienced, or in tough financial situations. Knowing how to spot and avoid them is one of the most important money skills you can learn.

Scams usually try to trick you into giving away money or personal information. They often come disguised as offers that sound too good to be true, or with messages that pressure you to act immediately. Some will ask for payment in unusual forms such as gift cards, wire transfers, or cryptocurrency. Others claim you have won a prize but demand that you pay fees before you can receive it. If something feels off, the best response is to slow down, research carefully, and verify before doing anything.

Predatory lending is another danger. This happens when lenders take advantage of people by charging extremely high interest rates, hidden fees, or unfair terms. Payday loans, rent-to-own stores, and certain "no credit check" loans are common examples. These can trap people in cycles of debt, making it nearly impossible to pay off what they owe.

The best protection is to be cautious before borrowing. Always read the terms closely and make sure you understand how much the loan will really cost. Comparing options is also wise, as credit unions and banks usually provide safer and more affordable loans. Building even a small emergency fund can keep you from having to turn to high-interest debt in a crisis. Above all, trust your instincts: if a deal feels sketchy or too good to be true, it probably is.

Avoiding scams and predatory lending is not just about saving money; it is about protecting your financial freedom and peace of mind.

Big Purchases: Cars, Appliances, Electronics

Some of the biggest financial decisions young adults face are buying cars, household appliances, or expensive electronics. These purchases can be exciting, but they are also situations where mistakes can cost a lot of money.

The most important rule is to avoid impulse buying. Large purchases should always be planned in advance, with time to compare prices, brands, and options. Marketing often makes you feel like you need the newest model or the most advanced features, but many times a slightly older or simpler version works just as well at a much lower cost.

When it comes to cars, think about the total cost of ownership, not just the sticker price. Fuel, insurance, maintenance, and repairs all add up over time. With appliances, focus on reliability and energy efficiency, since a cheaper product that breaks often or wastes electricity will cost more in the long run. For electronics like phones, laptops, or TVs, consider whether you actually need the upgrade now or if your current device still meets your needs.

Financing options can also be a trap. Stores and dealerships may offer monthly payment plans that look affordable, but the interest or fees hidden in the contract can make the purchase far more expensive than paying upfront. If you do need financing, shop around for the best terms, and never agree to something you don't fully understand.

Big purchases are not just about spending money, they are about making choices that affect your lifestyle for years. Taking time to plan, compare, and evaluate helps ensure you buy what you truly need without draining your finances.

12.

Government & the Economy (Practical View)

How Government Spending and Taxes Affect You

It can be easy to feel like government spending and taxes are distant issues that only politicians or big corporations need to worry about. In reality, they affect your daily life more than you might realize.

Taxes collected by the government (whether from income, sales, or property) are the main source of money used to run public services. These services include things you rely on every day, such as roads, schools, public transportation, healthcare systems, and safety through police and fire departments. In other words, a portion of your paycheck and every purchase you make helps fund the infrastructure and services that keep society running.

Government spending also plays a role in shaping the economy. When the government spends more money on things like building highways, funding research, or supporting education, it creates jobs and puts money into circulation. On the other hand, when governments cut back on spending, it can slow down economic growth, which sometimes leads to fewer jobs or reduced services.

The balance between spending and collecting taxes is a constant challenge. If the government spends more than it collects, it goes into debt, which can lead to higher taxes or reduced benefits in the future. If it collects more than it spends, it may ease debt but could also limit public investment in areas like healthcare, education, or infrastructure.

For everyday people, this balance influences the quality of services you receive, the taxes you pay, and the economic opportunities available in your community. Understanding this connection helps you see that government policies are not just abstract debates. They shape your personal finances and daily life in very real ways.

Inflation, Recessions, and Interest Rates Explained Simply

The economy can feel like a complicated machine, but at its core, it runs on money moving between people, businesses, and the government. Three key concepts: inflation, recessions, and interest rates, show how the economy affects your daily life.

Inflation happens when prices rise over time. A cup of coffee that costs two dollars today might cost three dollars in a few years. This doesn't mean the coffee is better; it means the value of money has gone down. A little inflation is normal and even healthy for the economy, but when prices rise too quickly, your paycheck doesn't stretch as far, making it harder to afford the same things.

A recession is the opposite problem. It happens when the economy slows down for months or even years. People buy less, businesses make less money, and some may close or lay off workers. During a recession, jobs can be harder to find and wages may stagnate. While tough to live through, recessions are a natural part of the economic cycle, and economies usually recover over time.

Interest rates are set by central banks (like the Federal Reserve in the United States). They control how cheap or expensive it is to borrow money. When interest rates are low, people and businesses can borrow more cheaply, which encourages spending and growth. But if inflation gets too high, central banks raise interest rates, which makes loans more expensive and slows down spending. This can cool the economy but also risks triggering a slowdown or recession.

For individuals, these concepts show up in everyday life: inflation means your groceries or rent cost more, recessions can impact your job security, and interest rates determine how much you pay on credit cards, student loans, or mortgages. Understanding these forces helps you see that the broader economy is not abstract. It directly shapes your budget, savings, and future opportunities.

Social Programs (Unemployment, Pensions, Healthcare, Welfare)

Governments don't just collect taxes and build roads. They also provide support systems called social programs. These programs are designed to help people when life doesn't go as planned or when extra support is needed.

Unemployment benefits provide temporary income to people who lose their jobs through no fault of their own. This safety net helps them cover basic expenses while searching for new work. Without it, a sudden job loss could push many families into financial crisis.

Pensions and retirement programs are designed to give people income after they stop working. In some countries, this comes from government-run systems like Social Security in the United States. In others, the government may require or encourage individuals to contribute to retirement accounts during their working years. These programs make sure that people aren't left without support in old age.

Healthcare programs vary widely by country, but they are aimed at making medical care more affordable and accessible. Some governments provide free or low-cost healthcare, while others subsidize private insurance. The goal is to prevent medical costs from bankrupting families when illness or accidents strike.

Welfare and assistance programs are broader forms of support for people facing financial hardship. These can include food assistance, housing aid, or cash benefits to help cover essentials. While sometimes controversial, these programs are often the difference between survival and poverty for vulnerable families.

For everyday people, social programs are a reminder that taxes don't just disappear into thin air. They come back in the form of protection, support, and opportunities that individuals might not be able to afford on their own. Even if you don't use these programs right now, knowing they exist adds a layer of security to your financial life.

13.

Global Economy Basics

Trade, Imports, Exports (Why It Affects Prices)

No country produces everything its people need. That's where trade comes in. Nations buy and sell goods and services across borders through imports and exports. Exports are what a country sells to others, while imports are what it buys. This constant flow of goods keeps shelves stocked, factories running, and economies growing.

Trade affects prices more than most people realize. When a country imports goods cheaply (say, clothing from factories overseas), consumers benefit because they can buy affordable products. But if something disrupts trade, such as tariffs, wars, natural disasters, or shipping delays, the cost of those goods can rise quickly. That's why electronics, cars, or even basic groceries sometimes suddenly become more expensive.

Exports also influence prices at home. If a country sells a lot of a product abroad, there may be less of it available domestically, which can push up local prices. For example, when global demand for grain rises, bread and cereal might cost more in the exporting country.

Trade creates variety and lowers costs, but it also makes economies interconnected. A shortage or crisis in one part of the world can ripple through and raise prices everywhere. For consumers, understanding this explains why prices at the store don't just depend on local conditions. They're shaped by global supply and demand.

Currency Exchange

Every country has its own currency, like the US dollar, the euro, or the Japanese yen. Currency exchange is the process of converting one type of money into another so that people and businesses can trade across borders.

The value of a currency is not fixed; It rises and falls depending on how much people want to use it. If a country's economy is strong, investors may prefer holding its currency, which makes it more valuable compared to others. On the other hand, if confidence in an economy drops, its currency may lose value.

For everyday people, currency exchange matters in more ways than just traveling abroad. If your country's currency becomes weaker, imported goods become more expensive, since it takes more local money to buy the same amount from another country. This can raise prices for electronics, clothing, fuel, or even food. On the flip side, if your currency strengthens, imports become cheaper, but exports might suffer because foreign buyers now see your goods as more expensive.

Businesses are heavily affected too. A car manufacturer that imports parts from abroad must watch exchange rates carefully, since even small changes can significantly affect costs and profits.

In short, currency exchange is like the world's financial balancing act. It determines how much your money is really worth outside your own country and influences the prices of many products you buy every day.

Why Gas Prices, Food, and Rent Fluctuate

One of the most frustrating parts of managing money is that the cost of essentials like gas, food, and housing never seems stable. These price changes aren't random. They are influenced by a mix of global and local factors.

Gas prices often change because oil is traded globally. Political tensions, natural disasters, or changes in supply and demand can cause the price of crude oil to rise or fall, and those changes are quickly reflected at the pump. Even small shifts in global oil production can make a noticeable difference in what you pay to fill your tank.

Food prices can swing for several reasons. Weather conditions like droughts, floods, or heat waves can reduce harvests, making certain foods more expensive. Transportation costs, which are tied to fuel prices, also affect what food costs by the time it reaches the store. On top of that, global demand plays a role: if more countries start buying the same crops, prices rise everywhere.

Rent is driven more by local conditions than global ones. The biggest factors are how many people need housing in an area and how many homes are available. If more people move to a city for jobs but housing construction doesn't keep up, rents go up. Interest rates can also influence rent, because when buying a home becomes more expensive due to higher mortgage costs, more people rent instead of buy, pushing demand for rentals higher.

These fluctuations can feel out of your control, but understanding why they happen makes them less mysterious. Global events, local supply and demand, and broader economic shifts all play a part in shaping the costs of everyday life.

14.

Planning for the Future

Retirement Planning

It may feel strange to think about retirement when you're just starting out in adult life, but planning early makes a huge difference later. Retirement planning is simply preparing for the time when you'll no longer earn a paycheck and will instead rely on savings, investments, or pensions to cover your living expenses.

The biggest reason to start early is the power of compound interest. Money that you save and invest in your twenties or thirties has decades to grow, which means small, steady contributions can turn into a large nest egg over time. Waiting until your forties or fifties means you'll have to save much larger amounts to reach the same goal.

Retirement savings can take different forms depending on where you live. In some countries, there are government programs like Social Security or state pensions, but these usually aren't enough to fully cover expenses. That's why most people also save through retirement accounts offered by employers or available individually, such as 401(k)s, IRAs, or similar regional equivalents. Employers sometimes match a portion of your contributions, which is essentially free money you don't want to miss.

A good retirement plan balances safety and growth. Early on, you can afford to take more risk by investing in stocks or funds that have the potential for higher returns. As you get closer to retirement age, it's wise to shift toward safer investments like bonds to protect what you've built.

The key is consistency. Even if you can only save a small amount each month, starting early and sticking with it will put you in a much stronger position later. Retirement planning isn't about getting rich. It's about ensuring you have financial freedom and security when you stop working.

Saving for Education, Home, or Major Goals

Life comes with big milestones that require big money: things like going to college, buying a home, starting a family, or funding personal dreams. These goals can feel overwhelming, but saving for them becomes manageable when you plan ahead.

The first step is to define the goal clearly. For example, maybe you want to buy a home in five years, pay for your child's education in fifteen, or take a year off to travel Each goal has a different time frame and cost, which influences how you should save.

For short-term goals, like buying a car or making a down payment on a home, keeping money in a high-yield savings account or a certificate of deposit is safer, since you don't want to risk losing your savings to stock market swings. For long-term goals, like education for children or your own retirement, investing in stocks, bonds, or mutual funds may make more sense because you have time to ride out market ups and downs while letting your money grow.

The key is to set aside money consistently. Treat it like a bill you pay yourself, even if it's only a small amount. Over time, those contributions add up. Automating transfers from your paycheck or checking account into a savings or investment account makes it easier to stay disciplined.

Big goals don't have to feel impossible. Breaking them into smaller, steady savings steps not only makes them realistic but also helps you stay motivated as you watch your progress build. Saving is less about sacrifice and more about giving your future self the resources to live the life you want.

Estate Planning: Wills, Inheritance Basics

Estate planning might sound like something only wealthy people need to worry about, but it's actually an important step for anyone who owns property, has savings, or cares about what happens to their belongings after they're gone. In simple terms, estate planning is deciding who will receive your assets and how your affairs will be handled when you pass away.

The most basic part of estate planning is a will. A will is a legal document that states who gets your money, property, and possessions, and who will take care of any dependents you have, such as children. Without a will, those decisions are left to the government, which can create confusion and delay for your loved ones. Writing a will ensures that your wishes are respected and your family avoids unnecessary legal stress.

Another important piece is choosing an executor: the person who will make sure your instructions are carried out. This should be someone you trust, who is organized and responsible. For people with more complex assets, such as a business or multiple properties, lawyers or financial advisors can help create more detailed estate plans, including trusts or tax strategies to protect what you've built.

Estate planning also involves reviewing beneficiary designations on accounts like insurance policies, retirement funds, or bank accounts. These forms determine who receives the money directly and sometimes override what's written in a will, so they need to be kept up to date.

Though it can be uncomfortable to think about, estate planning is one of the most caring things you can do for the people you leave behind. It provides clarity, prevents conflict, and ensures your life's work and savings go exactly where you want them to.

15.

Everyday Economic Survival Skills

Negotiation Basics

Negotiation is one of the most valuable life skills you can learn, and it's not just for business deals. You use it when you discuss salary, buy a car, rent an apartment, or even decide on responsibilities with roommates. Knowing how to negotiate well can save you money, earn you more, and help you get treated fairly.

The key to good negotiation is preparation. Before entering any discussion, know exactly what you want, what you're willing to compromise on, and what your limits are. For example, if you're negotiating rent, research average prices in the area so you can argue from a position of knowledge. If you're asking for a raise, gather examples of how you've added value to your workplace.

Confidence also matters. Speak calmly and clearly, and don't be afraid of silence, because it often gives the other person room to reconsider their position. Listen carefully to what the other side says, because understanding their priorities helps you find common ground.

Negotiation isn't about being aggressive or manipulative. It's about reaching a fair outcome where both sides feel satisfied. Even small negotiations can have a big impact on your finances over time. Saving a little here, earning a little more there - all of it adds up.

Learning to negotiate effectively helps you stand up for yourself, make smarter decisions, and feel more in control of your financial life.

Understanding Contracts

Contracts are a part of everyday life, even if you don't always notice them. When you sign a lease, start a new job, get a phone plan, or buy something online that requires you to "agree to terms," you're entering into a contract. At its core, a contract is a legally binding agreement between two or more parties that outlines what each side promises to do.

Understanding contracts is about protecting yourself. Once you sign, you're legally responsible for following the terms, even if you didn't read them carefully. That's why it's crucial to take your time before agreeing to anything. Read every section, including the fine print, because that's where important details are often hidden, such as fees, cancellation rules, or automatic renewals.

Good contracts are clear about the responsibilities of each party, payment amounts, deadlines, and what happens if someone breaks the agreement. If anything is vague or confusing, ask for clarification or request the terms in plain language. Never let anyone rush you into signing. If a company or person pressures you, that's usually a red flag.

You don't need to be a lawyer to understand contracts. You just need patience and attention to detail. If the agreement involves large sums of money, long-term commitments, or unfamiliar legal terms, it's wise to have a professional review it before signing.

By learning how to read and question contracts, you avoid unfair situations and keep control over your financial and personal commitments. It's a skill that builds confidence and helps you make informed, responsible choices.

Time Value of Money

One of the most powerful ideas in personal finance is the time value of money: the concept that money today is worth more than the same amount in the future. This is because money has the potential to grow over time through saving, investing, or earning interest.

Imagine someone gives you the choice between receiving $100 today or $100 a year from now. The smart choice is to take the money now, because you could put it in a savings account, invest it, or use it to create more value. If that $100 earns 5% interest, it becomes $105 after a year. Waiting a year to receive it means losing that growth opportunity.

This principle explains why starting to save and invest early matters so much. The earlier you begin, the more time your money has to grow. Even small, regular contributions can turn into a large sum thanks to compound interest: the process where your interest also earns interest over time.

The time value of money also helps you make better spending decisions. For instance, buying something on credit now means paying more later due to interest, which can make that item much more expensive in the long run. Thinking in terms of time value encourages you to ask: *Is this purchase worth giving up what my money could earn if I saved or invested it instead?*

Understanding this simple idea changes how you see money. It teaches you that time is a powerful financial tool, and the sooner you put your money to work, the more it can do for you.

Critical Thinking for Financial Decisions

When it comes to money, emotions often try to take the lead. Advertisements, social pressure, and fear of missing out can all push us toward decisions that might not actually make financial sense. That's why critical thinking is such an important skill for managing your finances wisely.

Critical thinking means slowing down to analyze information before acting. It involves asking questions like:

- *What are the real costs and benefits?*
- *Who stands to gain from this deal?*
- *Is this information based on facts or marketing?*
- *What's the long-term impact of this decision?*

For example, when you see a "limited-time offer," your instinct might be to buy quickly before the deal disappears. But critical thinking reminds you to check if the discount is real, compare prices elsewhere, and determine whether you truly need the item.

This skill also applies to bigger decisions like taking a loan, investing, or changing jobs. Instead of reacting emotionally or based on what others are doing, you evaluate evidence (interest rates, risks, timelines, and potential returns) to make a reasoned choice.

Critical thinking helps protect you from scams, predatory lending, and impulsive purchases. It keeps you grounded in facts, not feelings. By developing this mindset, you turn financial decision-making from a guessing game into a process guided by logic and understanding.

In short, critical thinking turns financial survival into financial confidence. It's the tool that helps you see through the noise and make decisions that truly serve your future.

Money doesn't have to be complicated. It's simply a tool, one that can either control you or serve you.

By understanding how it works, you gain more than financial security; you gain freedom. The freedom to make choices that fit *your* life, your goals, and your values.

So take what you've learned, start where you are, and remember: every smart decision, no matter how small, moves you closer to the life you want to build.

Your financial future starts today.

"Do not save what is left after spending, but spend what is left after saving."

Warren Buffett

www.ingramcontent.com/pod-product-compliance
Lightning Source LLC
LaVergne TN
LVHW090413210926
848480LV00002B/546